Signing at Home

SIGN LANGUAGE FOR KIDS

by Kathryn Clay
illustrated by Randy Chewning

Consultant: Kari Sween
Adjunct Instructor of
American Sign Language
Minnesota State University, Mankato

CAPSTONE PRESS
a capstone imprint

TABLE OF CONTENTS

How to Use This Guide

This book is full of useful words in both English and American Sign Language (ASL). The English word and sign for each word appear next to the picture. Arrows are used to show movement for some signs.

Most ASL signs are understood wherever you go. But some signs may change depending on where you are. It's like having a different accent.

For example, New Yorkers sign "pizza" like this:

People in other places might sign "pizza" like this:

or this:

People will not understand you if they can't see your signs. Make sure your hands are always in view when signing with someone. Don't be afraid to ask people to slow down or sign again if you don't understand a sign.

Brief Introduction to American Sign Language (ASL)

Many people who are deaf or hard of hearing use ASL to talk. Hearing people may also learn ASL to communicate with deaf friends and family members.

Signs can be very different from one another. Signs may use one or both hands. Sometimes signs have more than one step. For other signs, you must move your entire body. If there is no sign for a word, you can fingerspell it.

People use facial expressions when they sign. They smile when signing good news. They frown when signing sad news. Body language is also important. Someone might sign slowly to show that he or she is very tired.

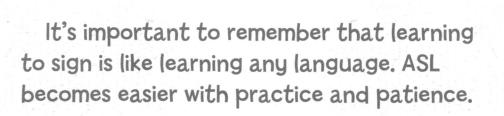

It's important to remember that learning to sign is like learning any language. ASL becomes easier with practice and patience.

Alphabet Chart

ASL has a sign for every letter of the English alphabet. If there is no sign for a word, you can use letter signs to spell out the word. Fingerspelling is often used to sign the names of people and places.

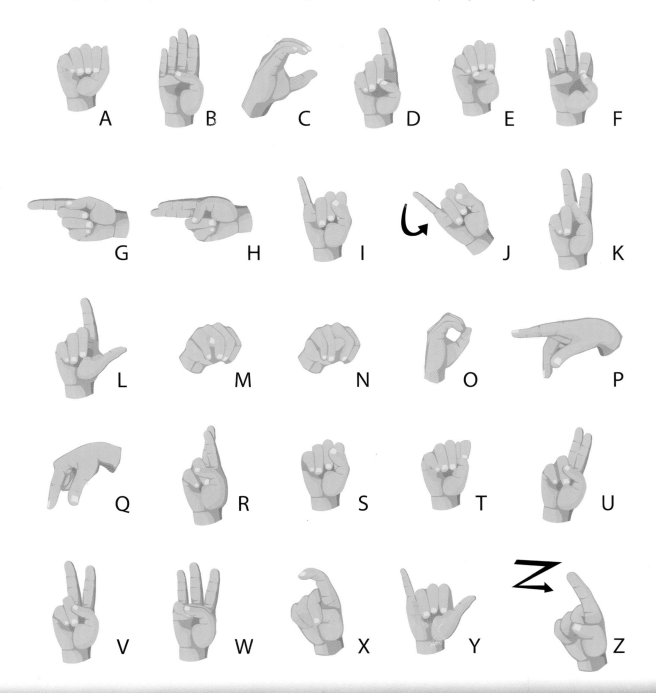

MY HOME

Move hand up cheek.

apartment Fingerspell A-P-T.

mailbox
1. Bring thumb to palm.
2. Make a box shape.

window Bring hands together.

door Twist hand to side.

garage Move bottom hand forward twice.

roof Touch fingertips. Move fingers away.

BEDROOM

1. Place hand on cheek.
2. Make a box shape.

dresser Move fists forward and down.

bed Place hand on cheek.

blanket Bring hands to shoulders.

8

pillow
Bring hand up twice.

book
Open hands like opening a book.

desk
Tap arms together twice.

computer
Slide C shape up arm.

CLOTHES

Slide hands down and out.

pants   Bring hands up twice.

shorts   Slide hands to sides.

socks   Rub fingers together.

shoes
Bring fists together.

hat
Pat head twice.

pajamas
1. Close hand in front of face.
2. Slide hands down and out.

shirt
Grab shirt and pull.

coat
Bring fists together.

TOYS

Fingerspell T-O-Y-S.

ball Bring fingers together.

train Slide fingers back and forth.

12

doll Slide finger down nose.

puzzle Lock fingers together.

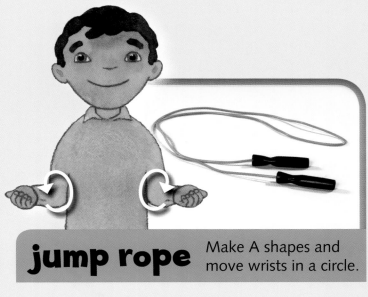

jump rope Make A shapes and move wrists in a circle.

game Make A shapes and tap knuckles together twice.

KITCHEN

Move K shape side to side.

refrigerator
Fingerspell R-E-F.

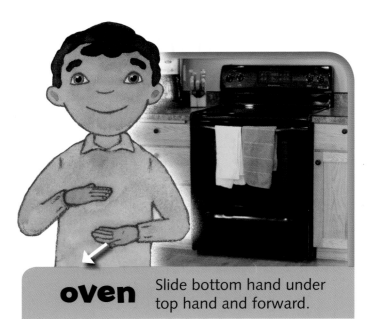

oven
Slide bottom hand under top hand and forward.

sink Fingerspell S-I-N-K.

microwave Open fists.

cook Move hand back and forth.

garbage can Move finger from wrist to elbow.

DINING ROOM

1. Bring hand to mouth.
2. Make a box shape.

spoon — Scoop fingers toward mouth.

fork — Slide fingers across palm.

knife — Slide top finger along bottom finger in a cutting motion.

16

table
Tap arms together twice.

cup
Make C shape and bring hand to palm.

plate
Bring wrists together in a circle.

bowl
Bring hands to the side.

FOOD

Touch fingers to mouth twice.

milk Squeeze fingers together.

bread Slide fingers across knuckles.

butter Slide fingers across palm twice.

fruit Wiggle F shape at chin.

cookie Rotate C shape.

vegetable Wiggle V shape at chin.

BATHROOM

Wiggle T shape.

towel Move fists back and forth.

bathtub
1. Slide hands up chest.
2. Fingerspell T-U-B.

soap Brush fingers against palm.

comb Bend fingers. Move hand back and forth.

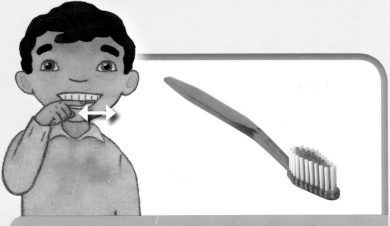

toothbrush Slide finger back and forth.

toilet Wiggle T shape.

mirror Wiggle hand in front of face.

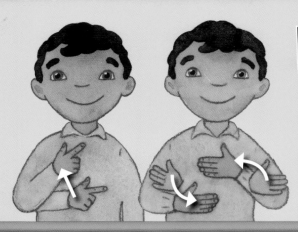

LIVING ROOM

1. Make L shape and slide hand up chest.
2. Make a box shape.

chair   Touch fingers together and tap twice.

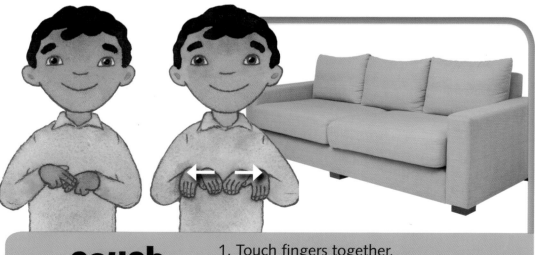

couch
1. Touch fingers together.
2. Make C shapes and slide out.

TV Fingerspell T-V.

light Open fist.

floor Slide hands to sides.

telephone Bring hand to cheek.

OUTDOORS

Tap shoulder twice.

flower   Move hand across face.

tree   Wiggle wrist back forth.

garden   Make G shape. Move hand up arm and in a circle.

dirt Rub fingers together.

bug Put thumb on nose and bend fingers.

shovel Make digging motion.

butterfly Connect thumbs and wave hands.

FAMILY

Make F shapes and move hands in a circle.

baby Rock arms back and forth.

mother Touch thumb to chin.

father Touch thumb to forehead.

brother

1. Place thumb on forehead.
2. Bring wrists together.

sister

1. Slide thumb along cheek.
2. Bring wrists together.

grandfather

1. Make the sign for "father."
2. Bounce hand away from forehead.

grandmother

1. Make the sign for "mother."
2. Bounce hand away from chin.

uncle
Move U shape in a circle.

aunt
Move A shape in a circle.

cousin
Shake C shape by side of head.

PETS

Rub hand twice.

dog   Pat leg. Snap fingers.

cat   Pretend to pull whiskers on face.

bird   Open and close fingers.

mouse Brush finger across nose.

snake Bend fingers and slide back and forth.

turtle Stick out thumb. Cover hand and wiggle thumb.

rabbit Cross hands. Move fingers up and down.

fish Hold hand sideways and wiggle.

GLOSSARY

accent—the way people say words differently based on where they live

body language—the act of sharing information by using gestures, movements, and facial expressions

communicate—to share thoughts, feelings, or information

deaf—unable to hear

facial expression—feelings shared by making different faces; making an angry face to show you are mad, for example

BOOKS IN THIS SERIES

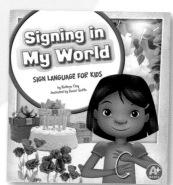

READ MORE

Nelson, Michiyo. *Sign Language: My First 100 Words.*
New York: Scholastic, 2008.

Petelinsek, Kathleen, and E. Russell Primm. *Home.*
Talking Hands. Chanhassen, Minn.: The Child's World, 2006.

Schaefer, Lola M. *Some Kids Are Deaf.*
Mankato, Minn.: Capstone Press, 2008.

INTERNET SITES

FactHound offers a safe, fun way to find Internet sites related to this book. All of the sites on FactHound have been researched by our staff.

Here's all you do:

Visit *www.facthound.com*

Type in this code: 9781620650516

Super-cool stuff! Check out projects, games and lots more at **www.capstonekids.com**

A+ Books are published by Capstone Press,
1710 Roe Crest Drive, North Mankato, Minnesota 56003
www.capstonepub.com

Library of Congress Cataloging-in-Publication Data
Clay, Kathryn.
  Signing at home : sign language for kids / by Kathryn Clay.
    pages cm.—(A+ books. Time to sign)
Summary: "Illustrations of American Sign Language, along with labeled photos,
introduce children to words and phrases useful for signing around their home"—Provided by publisher.
  ISBN 978-1-62065-051-6 (library binding)
  ISBN 978-1-4765-3356-8 (ebook PDF)
1. American Sign Language—Juvenile literature. 2. English language—Alphabet—Juvenile literature. I. Title.
  HV2480.C533 2014
  372.6—dc23   2013010643

Editorial Credits
Tracy Davies McCabe, designer; Svetlana Zhurkin, media researcher;
Kathy McColley, production specialist

Photo Credits
Capstone Studio: Karon Dubke, cover (middle right), 7, 8 (bottom left), 9 (top, middle, and bottom right), 10 (bottom), 11
(top left and bottom left), 12 (top), 13 (top left, bottom right, and bottom left), 14 (bottom), 15 (top left and top right), 17
(top left and bottom right), 18 (bottom), 19 (top left and bottom left), 20 (top), 21 (bottom left), 24 (middle and bottom), 25,
28 (top), 29 (top left, top right, and bottom left); iStockphotos: Bastun, 3, 5; Shutterstock: a40757, 6 (top), Africa Studio, 23
(top right), Andrey_Kuzmin, 26 (top), Andrey_Popov, 23 (top left), Artazum, 14 (top), Atiketta Sangasaeng, 22 (bottom),
B. and E. Dudzinscy, 19 (bottom right), Big Pants Production, 21 (top left), bloomua, 23 (bottom right), Carlos Moura, 12
(bottom), Coprid, 11 (top right), cynoclub, 28 (middle), gillmar, 17 (top right), icyimage, 20 (bottom), inxti, 17 (bottom
left), Irina Rogova, 10 (middle), Irina Tischenko, 16 (bottom), Joe Belanger, 6 (bottom), jordache, 29 (bottom right),
karamysh, cover (top left), Karkas, 11 (bottom right), Kasia Bialasiewicz, 9 (bottom left), Kitch Bain, 16 (middle),
majeczka, 24 (top), Mathisa, 15 (bottom right), Mikhail Dudarev, 19 (top right), Monkey Business Images,
26 (bottom), 27, neelsky, 18 (top), nito, 11 (middle), Orange Line Media, 15 (bottom left), Photoseeker,
16 (top), Robert Milek, 21 (bottom right), Santiago Cornejo, 23 (bottom left), Sara Robinson, 28
(bottom), shippee, 10 (top), sommthink, 8 (top), Twin Design, 29 (middle), Vaidas Bucys, 13 (top
right), Viktor1, 8 (bottom right), Vladimir Suponev, cover (bottom right), Vladyslav Danilin, 21
(middle), William Milner, 22 (top), yencha, 21 (top right)

Note to Parents, Teachers, and Librarians
This accessible, visual guide uses full color photographs and illustrations
and inviting content to introduce young readers to American Sign Language.
The book provides an early introduction to reference materials and encourages
further learning by including the following sections: Table of Contents, Alphabet
Chart, Glossary, Read More, and Internet Sites.

Printed in the United States of America in North Mankato, Minnesota.
032013   007223CGF13